IT CAN BE DONE
Poems for Hardship, Sacrifice and Dominion

IT CAN BE DONE
Poems for Hardship, Sacrifice and Dominion

Edited by:

Scott T. Brown

The NATIONAL CENTER *for*
FAMILY-INTEGRATED CHURCHES

Second Printing: August 2014
First Printing: November 2009

Copyright © 2014 by The National Center for Family-Integrated Churches. All rights reserved. No part of this book may be used or reproduced in any manner whatsoever without written permission of the publisher, except in the case of brief quotations in articles and reviews.

The National Center for Family-Integrated Churches
220 South White St. Wake Forest North Carolina 27587
www.ncfic.org

ISBN - 0-9820567-6-1
ISBN - 978-0-9820567-6-9

Book Design By David Edward Brown

Printed in the United States of America

TABLE OF CONTENTS

Foreword 15

It Couldn't Be Done 19
- Edger A. Guest

Be the Best of Whatever You Are 21
- Douglas Malloch

See It Through 22
- Edger A. Guest

When God* Wants a Man 24
- Angela Morgan

Victory 28
- Miriam Teichner

Keep on Keepin' On 29
- Anonymous

The Welcome Man 30	
- Walt Mason	
Wanted - A Man 32	
- St. Clair Adams	
Work 34	
- Angela Morgan	
How Did You Die? 37	
- Edmund Vance Cooke	
A Lesson From History 39	
- Joseph Morris	
Worth While 40	
-Ella Wheeler Wilcox	
Hope 42	
- Anonymous	
Might have Been 43	
-Grantland Rice	
There Will Always Be Something to Do 44	
- Edgar A. Guest	
How Do You Tackle Your Work? 46	
- Edgar A. Guest	
Opportunity 47	
-Walter Malone	
Opportunity 49	
-Edward Rowland Sill	

Preparedness..50
-Edwin Markham

Life and Death..50
-Ernest H. Crosby

The Things that Haven't Been Done Before..................52
- Edgar A. Guest

Can't...54
-Edgar A. Guest

The Firm of Grin and Barrett..............................56
-Sam Walter Foss

Unafraid..58
-Everard Jack Appleton

The Trainers...59
-Grantland Rice

Battle Cry..61
-John G. Neihardt

If You Can't Go Over or Under, Go Around..................62
- Joseph Morris

A Prayer..64
-Theodosia Garrison

The Man Who Frets at Worldly Strife.......................66
-Joseph Rodman Drake

Heinelet..67
-Gamaliel Bradford

On Down the Road..68
-Grantland Rice

Co-Operation...69
-J. Mason Knox

Four Things..69
-Henry Van Dyke

If..70
-Rudyard Kipling

The Lion Path..72
-Charlotte Perkins Gilman

Good Intentions..74
-St. Clair Adams

The Fighting Failure.....................................75
-Everard Jack Appleton

My Philosophy..78
-James Whitcomb Riley

Work...79
- Henry Van Dyke

Wishing..80
-Ella Wheeler Wilcox

To the Men Who Lose......................................82
- Anonymous

Your Mission	83
-Ellen M. H. Gates	
Borrowed Feathers	85
-Joseph Morris	
A Poor Unfortunate	87
-Frank L. Stanton	
Clear the Way	88
-Charles Mackay	
Thick Is the Darkness	90
-William Ernest Henley	
Cleon and I	91
-Charles Mackay	
Meetin' Trouble	93
-Everard Jack Appleton	
My Creed	94
-S. E. Kiser	
Borrowing Trouble	96
-Robert Burns	
Character of a Happy Life	96
-Sir Henry Wotton	

Slogan 98
-Jane M'Lean

Smiles 99
-Ella Wheeler Wilcox

Keep A-goin'! 101
-Frank L. Stanton

The House by the Side of the Road 102
-Sam Walter Foss

FOREWORD

My first exposure to these poems came when I arrived home one day and was met by my wife Deborah at the door. With book in hand, she began to read poems with the express purpose of inspiring me. The first poem she read was, "It Couldn't Be Done," and I was hooked.

These poems are about real life. They will make you smile, square your jaw, lighten your load, heighten your step, and grow rebar in your spine. They will lift you up, make you soar, and give you a view of the smallness of your problems. They will help you think bigger, feel better, laugh harder, and eat your problems for breakfast.

The book was originally published in 1921 and contained 239 poems. I have cut these down to my favorites - the ones my wife read to me in her quest to be a good helper to her husband by inspiring him that, "It Can Be Done!"

This is a book for the rescue of 21st Century manhood and womanhood. The world needs real men and women today.

IT CAN BE DONE

Our world is sick with feminized, soft, mollycoddling, sensitive males who are always looking for permission and affirmation and certification to do anything. These male maladies are ripping our culture apart. The average male today never grows up and rarely leads. He is an emotional basket case, constantly jerked around by his feelings - not governed by eternal principles. He is worried about his hair, spends his life playing games, and has a therapist. The result is that he settles for "whatever."

Our world needs real women as well. It is reeling under the influence of dizzy, ditzy women whose vision is centered around themselves. It is languishing at the hands of women whose energy and joy have dissolved under the pressures of life. Instead, we need strong women who refuse to be unraveled or frightened by any fear. The world is crying out for a new version of resolute visionary women who are able to rise above their disappointments to see the goal. They sacrifice their lives for their children and follow their men to the ends of the earth.

"It Can Be Done!" by those who look hardship in the face, ready themselves for sacrifice and engage themselves in dominion.

IT COULDN'T BE DONE

After a thing has been done, everybody is ready to declare it easy. But before it has been done, it is called impossible. One reason why people fear to embark upon great enterprises is that they see all the difficulties at once. They know they could succeed in the initial tasks, but they shrink from what is to follow. Yet "a thing begun is half done." Moreover the surmounting of the first barrier gives strength and ingenuity for the harder ones beyond. Mountains viewed from a distance seem to be unscalable. But they can be climbed, and the way to begin is to take the first upward step. From that moment the mountains are less high. As Hannibal led his army across the foothills, then among the upper ranges, and finally over the loftiest peaks and passes of the Alps, or as Peary pushed farther and farther into the solitudes that encompass the North Pole, so can you achieve any purpose whatsoever if you heed not the doubters, meet each problem as it arises, and keep ever with you the assurance, "It Can Be Done."

Somebody said that it couldn't be done,
But he with a chuckle replied
That "maybe it couldn't," but he would be one
Who wouldn't say so till he'd tried.
So he buckled right in with the trace of a grin
On his face. If he worried he hid it.

IT CAN BE DONE

He started to sing as he tackled the thing
That couldn't be done, and he did it.

Somebody scoffed: "Oh, you'll never do that;
At least no one ever has done it";
But he took off his coat and he took off his hat,
And the first thing we knew he'd begun it.
With a lift of his chin and a bit of a grin,
Without any doubting or quiddit,
He started to sing as he tackled the thing
That couldn't be done, and he did it.

There are thousands to tell you it cannot be done,
There are thousands to prophesy failure;
There are thousands to point out to you one by one
The dangers that wait to assail you.

But just buckle in with a bit of a grin,
Just take off your coat and go to it;
Just start to sing as you tackle the thing
That "cannot be done," and you'll do it.

EDGAR A. GUEST

IT CAN BE DONE

BE THE BEST OF WHATEVER YOU ARE

We all dream of great deeds and high positions, away from the pettiness and humdrum of ordinary life. Yet success is not occupying a lofty place or doing conspicuous work. Rattling around in too big a job is much worse than filling a small one to overflowing. Dream, aspire by all means; but do not ruin the life you must lead by dreaming pipe-dreams of the one you would like to lead. Make the most of what you have and are. Perhaps your trivial, immediate task is your one sure way of proving your mettle. Do the thing near at hand, and great things will come to your hand to be done.

If you can't be a pine on the top of the hill
Be a scrub in the valley - but be
The best little scrub by the side of the hill;
Be a bush if you can't be a tree.

If you can't be a bush be a bit of the grass,
And some highway some happier make;
If you can't be a muskie then just be a bass-
But the liveliest bass in the lake!

We can't all be captains, we've got to be crew,
There's something for all of us here.

IT CAN BE DONE

There's big work to do and there's lesser to do,
And the task we must do is the near.

If you can't be a highway then just be a trail,
If you can't be the sun be a star;
It isn't by size that you win or you fail-
Be the best of whatever you are!

DOUGLAS MALLOCH

SEE IT THROUGH

An American traveler in Italy stood watching a lumberman who, as the logs floated down a swift mountain stream, jabbed his hook in an occasional one and drew it carefully aside. "Why do you pick out those few?" the traveler asked. "They all look alike." "But they are not alike, seignior. The logs I let pass have grown on the side of a mountain, where they have been protected all their lives. Their grain is coarse; they are good only for lumber. But these logs, seignior, grew on the top of the mountain. From the time they were sprouts and saplings they were lashed and buffeted by the winds, and so they grew strong with fine grain. We save them for choice work; they are not 'lumber', seignior."

IT CAN BE DONE

When you're up against a trouble,
Meet it squarely, face to face;
Lift your chin and set your shoulders,
Plant your feet and take a brace.
When it's vain to try to dodge it,
Do the best that you can do;
You may fail, but you may conquer,
See it through!

Black may be the clouds about you
And your future may seem grim,
But don't let your nerve desert you;
Keep yourself in fighting trim.
If the worse is bound to happen,
Spite of all that you can do,
Running from it will not save you,
See it through!

Even hope may seem but futile,
When with troubles you're beset,
But remember you are facing
Just what other men have met.
You may fail, but fall still fighting;
Don't give up, whate'er you do;

IT CAN BE DONE

Eyes front, head high to the finish.
See it through!

EDGAR A. GUEST

WHEN GOD* WANTS A MAN

Only melting and hammering can shape and temper steel for fine use. Only struggle and suffering can give a man the qualities that enable him to render large service to humanity.

When God wants to drill a man
And thrill a man,
And skill a man,
When God wants to mould a man
To play the noblest part;
When He yearns with all His heart
To create so great and bold a man
That all the world shall praise-
Watch His method, watch His ways!
How He ruthlessly perfects
Whom He royally elects;
How He hammers him and hurts him
And with mighty blows converts him

IT CAN BE DONE

Into trial shapes of clay which only God understands-
While his tortured heart is crying and he lifts beseeching hands!-
How He bends, but never breaks,
When his good He undertakes...
How He uses whom He chooses
And with every purpose fuses him,
By every art induces him
To try his splendor out-
God knows what He's about.

When God wants to take a man
And shake a man
And wake a man;
When God wants to make a man
To do the Father's will;
When He tries with all His skill
And He yearns with all His soul
To create him large and whole. . .
With what cunning He prepares him!
How He goads and never spares him,
How He whets him and He frets him
And in poverty begets him. . .
How He often disappoints
Whom He sacredly anoints,

IT CAN BE DONE

With what wisdom He will hide him,
Never minding what betide him
Though his genius sob with slighting and his
pride may not forget!
Bids him struggle harder yet.
Makes him lonely
So that only
God's high messages shall reach him
So that He may surely teach him
What the Hierarchy planned.
Though he may not understand
Gives him passions to command-
How remorselessly He spurs him,
With terrific ardor stirs him
When He poignantly prefers him!

When God wants to name a man
And fame a man
And tame a man;
When God wants to shame a man
To do his heavenly best...
When He tries the highest test
That His reckoning may bring-
When He wants a prince or king!-
How He reins him and restrains him
So his body scarce contains him

IT CAN BE DONE

While He fires him
And inspires him!

Keeps him yearning, ever burning for a
tantalizing goal-
Lures and lacerates his soul.
Sets a challenge for his spirit,
Draws it higher when he's near it -
Makes a jungle, that he clear it;
Makes a desert, that he fear it
And subdue it if he can-
So doth God make a man.
Then, to test his spirit's wrath
Hurls a mountain in his path-
Puts a bitter choice before him
And relentless stands o'er him.
"Climb, or perish!" so He says,
Watch His purpose, watch His ways!

God's plan is wondrous kind
Could we understand His mind.
Fools are they who call His blind.
When his feet are torn and bleeding
Yet his spirit mounts unheeding,
All his higher powers speeding
Blazing newer paths and fine;

IT CAN BE DONE

When the force that is divine
Leaps to challenge every failure and his ardor
still is sweet
And love and hope are burning in the presence
of defeat...
Lo, the crisis! Lo, the shout
That must call the leader out.
When the people need salvation
Doth he come to lead the nation
Then doth God show His plan
When the world has found a man!

ANGELA MORGAN

*The editors have replaced the author's original word "Nature" with "God".

VICTORY

To fail is not a disgrace; the disgrace lies in not trying. In his old age, Sir Walter Scott found that a publishing firm he was connected with was heavily in debt. He refused to take advantage of the bankruptcy law, and sat down with his pen to make good the deficit. Though he wore out his life in the struggle and did not live to see the debt entirely liquidated, he died an honored and honorable man.

IT CAN BE DONE

I call no fight a losing fight
If, fighting, I have gained some straight new strength;
If, fighting, I turned ever toward the light,
All unallied with forces of the night;
If, beaten, quivering, I could say at length:
"I did no deed that needs to be unnamed;
I fought - and lost - and I am unashamed."

MIRIAM TEICHNER

KEEP ON KEEPIN' ON

The author of these homely stanzas has caught perfectly the spirit which succeeds in the rough-and-tumble of actual life.

If the day looks kinder gloomy
And your chances kinder slim,
If the situation's puzzlin'
And the prospect's awful grim,
If perplexities keep pressin'
Till hope is nearly gone,
Just bristle up and grit your teeth
And keep on keep in' on.

IT CAN BE DONE

Frettin' never wins a fight
And fumin' never pays;
There ain't no use in broodin'
In these pessimistic ways;
Smile just kinder cheerfully
Though hope is nearly gone,
And bristle up and grit your teeth
And keep on keepin' on.

There ain't no use in growlin'
And grumblin' all the time,
When music's ringin' everywhere
And everything's a rhyme.
Just keep on smilin' cheerfully
If hope is nearly gone,
And bristle up and grit your teeth
And keep on keepin' on.

ANONYMOUS

THE WELCOME MAN

There's a man in the world who is never turned down,
Wherever he chances to stray;

IT CAN BE DONE

He gets the glad hand in the populous town,
Or out where the farmers make hay;
He's greeted with pleasure on deserts of sand,
And deep in the aisles of the woods;
Wherever he goes there's the welcoming hand
He's The Man Who Delivers the Goods.

The failures of life sit around and complain;
The gods haven't treated them right;
They've lost their umbrellas whenever there's rain,
And they haven't their lanterns at night;
Men tire of the failures who fill with their sighs
The air of their own neighborhoods;
There's one who is greeted with love-lighted eyes
He's The Man Who Delivers the Goods.

One fellow is lazy and watches the clock,
And waits for the whistle to blow;
And one has a hammer, with which he will knock,
And one tells a story of woe;
And one, if requested to travel a mile,
Will measure the perches and roods
But one does his stunt with a whistle or smile
He's The Man Who Delivers the Goods.

IT CAN BE DONE

One man is afraid that he'll labor too hard-
The world isn't yearning for such;
And one man is always alert, on his guard,
Lest he put in a minute too much;
And one has a grouch or a temper that's bad,
And one is a creature of moods;
So it's hey for the joyous and rollicking lad-
For the One Who Delivers the Goods!

WALT MASON

WANTED - A MAN

Business and the world are exacting in their demands upon us. They make no concessions to half-heartedness, incompetence, or plodding mediocrity. But for the man who has proved his worth and can do the exceptional things with originality and sound judgment, they are eagerly watchful and have rich rewards.

You say big corporations scheme
To keep a fellow down;
They drive him, shame him, starve him too
If he so much as frown.
God knows I hold no brief for them

IT CAN BE DONE

Still, come with me to-day
And watch those fat directors meet,
For this is what they say;

"In all our force not one to take
The new work that we plan!
In all the thousand men we've hired
Where shall we find a man?"

The world is shabby in the way
It treats a fellow too;
It just endures him while he works
And kicks him when he's through.
It's ruthless, yes; let him make good
Or else it grabs its broom
And grumbles: "What a clutter's here!
We can't have this. Make room!"

And out he goes. It says, "Can bread
Be made from mouldy bran?
The men come swarming here in droves
But where'll I find a man?"
Yes, life is hard. But all the same
It seeks the man who's best.
Its grudging makes the prizes big;
The obstacle's a test.

IT CAN BE DONE

Don't ask to find the pathway smooth,
To march to fife and drum;
The plum-tree will not come to you;
Jack Horner, hunt the plum.

The eyes of life are yearning, sad,
As humankind they scan.
She says, "Oh, there are men enough,
But where'll I find a man?"

ST. CLAIR ADAMS

WORK
"A SONG OF TRIUMPH"

When Captain John Smith was made the leader of the colonists at Jamestown, Va., he discouraged the get-rich-quick seekers of gold by announcing flatly, "He who will not work shall not eat." This rule made Jamestown the first permanent English settlement in the New World. But work does more than lead to material success. It gives an outlet from sorrow, restrains wild desires, ripens and refines character, enables human beings to cooperate with God, and when well done, brings to life its consummate satisfaction.

IT CAN BE DONE

Every man is a Prince of Possibilities, but by work alone can he come into his Kingship.

Work!
Thank God for the might of it,
The ardor, the urge, the delight of it-
Work that springs from the heart's desire,
Setting the brain and the soul on fire-
Oh, what is so good as the heat of it,
And what is so glad as the beat of it,
And what is so kind as the stern command,
Challenging brain and heart and hand?

Work!
Thank God for the pride of it,
For the beautiful, conquering tide of it,
Sweeping the life in its furious flood,
Thrilling the arteries, cleansing the blood,
Mastering stupor and dull despair,
Moving the dreamer to do and dare.
Oh, what is so good as the urge of it,
And what is so glad as the surge of it,
And what is so strong as the summons deep,
Rousing the torpid soul from sleep?

IT CAN BE DONE

Work!
Thank God for the pace of it,
For the terrible, keen, swift race of it;
Fiery steeds in full control,
Nostrils a-quiver to greet the goal.
Work the Power that drives behind,
Guiding the purposes, taming the mind,
Holding the runaway wishes back,
Reining the will to on steady track,
Speeding the energies faster, faster,
Triumphing over disaster.
Oh, what is so good as the pain of it,
And what is so great as the gain of it?
And what is so kind as the cruel goad,
Forcing us on through the rugged road?

Work!
Thank God for the swing of it,
For the clamoring, hammering ring of it,
Passion and labor daily hurled
On the mighty anvils of the world.
Oh what is so fierce as the flame of it?
And what is so huge as the aim of it?
Thundering on through dearth and doubt,
Calling the plan of the Maker out.
Work the Titan; Work, the friend,

IT CAN BE DONE

Shaping the earth to a glorious end,
Draining the swamps and blasting the hills,
Doing whatever the Spirit wills
Rending a continent apart,
To answer the dream of the Master heart.
Thank God for a world where none may shirk
Thank God for the splendor of work!

ANGELA MORGAN

HOW DID YOU DIE?

Grant at Ft. Donelson demanded unconditional and immediate surrender. At Appomattox he offered as lenient terms as victor ever extended to vanquished. Why the difference? The one event was at the beginning of the war, when the enemy's morale must be shaken. The other was at the end of the conflict, when a brave and noble adversary had been rendered helpless. Grant taught a great lesson. No honor can be too great for the man, be he even our foe, who has steadily and uncomplainingly done his very best - and has failed.

Did you tackle that trouble that came your way
With a resolute heart and cheerful?

IT CAN BE DONE

Or hide your face from the light of day
With a craven soul and fearful?
Oh, a trouble's a ton, or a trouble's an ounce,
Or a trouble is what you make it,
And it isn't the fact that you're hurt that counts,
But only how did you take it?

You are beaten to earth? Well, well, what's that!
Come up with a smiling face.
It's nothing against you to fall down flat,
But to lie there - that's disgrace.
The harder you're thrown, why the higher you bounce'
Be proud of your blackened eye!
It isn't the fact that you're licked that counts;
It's how did you fight - and why?

And though you be done to the death, what then?
If you battled the best you could,
If you played your part in the world of men,
Why, the Critic will call it good.
Death comes with a crawl, or comes with a pounce,
And whether he's slow or spry,
It isn't the fact that you're dead that counts,
But only how did you die?

EDMUND VANCE COOKE

IT CAN BE DONE

A LESSON FROM HISTORY

To break the ice of an undertaking is difficult. To cross on broken ice as Eliza did to freedom, or to row amid floating ice, as Washington did to victory, is harder still. This poem applies especially to those who are discouraged in a struggle to which they are already committed.

Everything's easy after it's done;
Every battle's a "cinch" that's won;
Every problem is clear that's solved-
The earth was round when it revolved!
But Washington stood amid grave doubt
With enemy forces camped about;
He could not know how he would fare
Till after he'd crossed the Delaware.
Though the river was full of ice
He did not think about it twice,
But started across in the dead of night,
The enemy waiting to open the fight.
Likely feeling pretty blue,
Being human, same as you,
But he was brave amid despair,
And Washington crossed the Delaware!
So when you're with trouble beset,
And your spirits are soaking wet,

IT CAN BE DONE

When all the sky with clouds is black,
Don't lie down upon your back
And look at them. Just do the thing;
Though you are choked, still try to sing.
If times are dark, believe them fair,
And you will cross the Delaware!

JOSEPH MORRIS

WORTH WHILE

A little boy whom his mother had rebuked for not turning a deaf ear to temptation protested, with tears, that he had no deaf ear. But temptation, even when heard, must somehow be resisted. Yea especially when heard! We deserve no credit for resisting it unless it comes to our ears like the voice of the siren.

It is easy enough to be pleasant,
When life flows by like a song,
But the man worth while is one who will smile
When everything goes dead wrong.
For the test of the heart is trouble
And it always comes with the years,

IT CAN BE DONE

And the smile that is worth the praises of earth.
Is the smile that shines through tears.

It is easy enough to be prudent,
When nothing tempts you to stray,
When without or within no voice of sin
Is luring your soul away;
But it's only a negative virtue
Until it is tried by fire,
And the life that is worth the honor on earth,
Is the one that resists desire.

By the cynic, the sad, the fallen,
Who had no strength for the strife
The world's highway is cumbered to-day,
They make up the sum of life.
But the virtue that conquers passion,
And the sorrow that hides in a smile
It is these that are worth the homage on earth
For we find them but once in a while.

ELLA WHEELER WILCOX

IT CAN BE DONE

HOPE

Gloom and despair are really ignorance in another form. They fail to reckon with the fact that what appears to be baneful often turns out to be good. Lincoln lost the senatorship to Douglas and thought he had ended his career; had he won the contest, he might have remained only a senator. Life often has surprise parties for us. Things come to us masked in gloom and black, but Time, the revealer, strips off the disguise, and lo, what we have is blessings.

Never go gloomy, man with a mind,
Hope is a better companion than fear;
Providence, ever benignant and kind,
Gives with a smile what you take with a tear;
All will be right,
Look to the light.
Morning was ever the daughter of night;
All that was black will be all that is bright,
Cheerily, cheerily, then cheer up.

Many a foe is a friend in disguise,
Many a trouble a blessing most true,
Helping the heart to be happy and wise,
With love ever precious and joy ever new.
Stand in the van,

IT CAN BE DONE

Strike like a man!
This is the bravest and cleverest plan;
Trusting in God while you do what you can.
Cheerily, cheerily, then cheer up.

ANONYMOUS

MIGHT HAVE BEEN

"Yes, it's pretty hard," the optimistic old woman admitted. "I have to get along with only two teeth, one in the upper jaw and one in the lower-but thank God, they meet."

Here's to "The days that might have been"
Here's to "The life I might have led"
The fame I might have gathered in-
The glory ways I might have sped.
Great "Might Have Been," I drink to you
Upon a throne where thousands hail-
And then - there looms another view-
I also "might have been" in jail.

O "Land of Might Have Been," we turn
With aching hearts to where you wait;
Where crimson fires of glory burn,

IT CAN BE DONE

And laurel crowns the guarding gate;
We may not see across your fields
The sightless skulls that knew their woe-
The broken spears - the shattered shields-
That "might have been" as truly so.

"Of all sad words of tongue or pen"-
So wails the poet in his pain-
The saddest are, "It might have been,"
And world-wide runs the dull refrain.
The saddest? Yes - but in the jar
This thought brings to me with its curse,
I sometimes think the gladdest are
"It might have been a blamed sight worse."

GRANTLAND RICE

THERE WILL ALWAYS BE SOMETHING TO DO

There will always be something to do, my boy;
There will always be wrongs to right;
There will always be need for a manly breed
And men unafraid to fight.

IT CAN BE DONE

There will always be honor to guard, my boy;
There will always be hills to climb,
And tasks to do, and battles new
From now till the end of time.

There will always be dangers to face, my boy;
There will always be goals to take;
Men shall be tried, when the roads divide,
And proved by the choice they make.
There will always be burdens to bear, my boy;
There will always be need to pray;
There will always be tears through the future years.
As loved ones are borne away.

There will always be God to serve, my boy,
And always the Flag above;
They shall call to you until life is through
For courage and strength and love.
So these are things that I dream, my boy,
And have dreamed since your life began:
That whatever befalls, when the old world calls,
It shall find you a sturdy man.

EDGAR A. GUEST

HOW DO YOU TACKLE YOUR WORK?

It would be foolish to begin digging a tunnel through a mountain with a mere pick and spade. We must assemble for the task great mechanical contrivances. And so with our energies of will; a slight tool means a slight achievement; a huge, aggressive engine, driving on at full blast, means corresponding bigness of results.

How do you tackle your work each day?
Are you scared of the job you find?
Do you grapple the task that comes your way
With a confident, easy mind?
Do you stand right up to the work ahead
Or fearfully pause to view it?
Do you start to toil with a sense of dread
Or feel that you're going to do it?
You can do as much as you think you can,
But you'll never accomplish more;
If you're afraid of yourself, young man,
There's little for you in store.
For failure comes from the inside first,
It's there if we only knew it,
And you can win, though you face the worst,
If you feel that you're going to do it.

IT CAN BE DONE

How do you tackle your work each day?
With confidence clear, or dread?
What to yourself do you stop and say
When a new task lies head?
What is the thought that is in your mind?
Is fear ever running through it?
If so, just tackle the next you find
By thinking you're going to do it.

EDGAR A. GUEST

OPPORTUNITY

No matter how a man may have failed in the past, the door of opportunity is always open to him.

They do me wrong who say I come no more
When once I knock and fail to find you in;
For every day I stand outside your door,
And bid you wake, and rise to fight and win.

Wail not for precious chances passed away,
Weep not for golden ages on the wane!

IT CAN BE DONE

Each night I burn the records of the day,
At sunrise every soul is born again!

Laugh like a boy at splendors that have sped,
To vanished joys be blind and deaf and dumb;
My judgments seal the dead past with its dead,
But never bind a moment yet to come.

Though deep in mire, wring not your hands and weep;
I lend my arm to all who say "I can!"
No shame-faced outcast ever sank so deep,
But yet might rise and be again a man!

Dost thou behold thy lost youth all aghast?
Dost reel from righteous Retribution's blow?
Then turn from blotted archives of the past,
And find the future's pages white as snow.

Art thou a mourner? Rouse thee from thy spell;
Art thou a sinner? Sins may be forgiven;
Each morning gives thee wings to flee from hell
Each night a star to guide thy feet to heaven.

WALTER MALONE

OPPORTUNITY

In this poem yet another view of opportunity is presented. The recreant or the dreamer complains that he has no real chance. He would succeed, he says, if he had but the implements of success - money, influence, social prestige, and the like. But success lies far less in implements than in the use we make of them. What one man throws away as useless, another man seizes as the best means of victory at hand. For everyone of us the materials for achievement are sufficient. The spirit that prompts us is what ultimately counts.

This I beheld, or dreamed it in a dream:
There spread a cloud of dust along a plain;
And underneath the cloud, or in it, raged
A furious battle, and men yelled, and swords
Shocked upon swords and shields. A prince's banner
Wavered, then staggered backward, hemmed by foes.

A craven hung along the battle's edge,
And thought, "Had I a sword of keener steel-
That blue blade that the king's son bears,-but this
Blunt thing!" he snapt and flung it from his hand,
And lowering crept away and left the field.

IT CAN BE DONE

Then came the king's son, wounded, sore bestead,
And weaponless, and saw the broken sword,
Hilt-buried in the dry and trodden sand,
And ran and snatched it, and with battle-shout
Lifted afresh he hewed his enemy down,
And saved a great cause that heroic day.

EDWARD ROWLAND SILL

PREPAREDNESS

For all your days prepare,
And meet them ever alike:
When you are the anvil, bear-
When you are the hammer, strike.

EDWIN MARKHAM

LIFE AND DEATH

Many a man would die for wife and children, for faith, for country. But would he live for them? That, often, is the more heroic course - and the more sensible. A rich man was hiring a driver for his carriage. He asked each applicant how close

IT CAN BE DONE

he could drive to a precipice without toppling over. "One foot," "Six inches," "Three inches," ran the replies. But an Irishman declared "Faith, and I'd keep as far away from the place as I could." "Consider yourself employed," was the rich man's comment.

So he died for his faith. That is fine,
More than most of us do.
But stay, can you add to that line
That he lived for it, too?
In death he bore witness at last
As a martyr to truth.
Did his life do the same in the past
From the days of his youth?

It is easy to die. Men have died
For a wish or a whim-
From bravado or passion or pride.
Was it harder for him?

But to live: every day to live out
All the truth that he dreamt,
While his friends met his conduct with doubt,
And the world with contempt-

IT CAN BE DONE

Was it thus that he plodded ahead,
Never turning aside?
Then we'll talk of the life that he led-
Never mind how he died.

ERNEST H. CROSBY

THE THINGS THAT HAVEN'T BEEN DONE BEFORE

It is said that if you hold a stick in front of the foremost sheep in a flock that files down a trail in the mountains, he will jump it-and that every sheep thereafter will jump when he reaches the spot, even if the stick be removed. So are many people mere unthinking imitators, blind to facts and opportunities about them. Kentucky could not be lived in by the white race till Daniel Boone built his cabin there. The air was not part of the domain of humanity till the Wright brothers made themselves birdmen.

The things that haven't been done before,
Those are the things to try;
Columbus dreamed of an unknown shore
At the rim of the far-flung sky,
And his heart was bold and his faith was strong

IT CAN BE DONE

As he ventured in dangers new,
And he paid no heed to the jeering throng
Or the fears of the doubting crew.

The many will follow the beaten track
With guideposts on the way,
They live and have lived for ages back
With a chart for every day.
Someone has told them it's safe to go
On the road he has traveled o'er,
And all that they ever strive to know
Are the things that were known before.

A few strike out, without map or chart,
Where never a man has been,
From the beaten paths they draw apart
To see what no man has seen.
There are deeds they hunger alone to do;
Though battered and bruised and sore,
They blaze the path for the many, who
Do nothing not done before.

The things that haven't been done before
Are the tasks worth while to-day;
Are you one of the flock that follows, or
Are you one that shall lead the way?

IT CAN BE DONE

Are you one of the timid souls that quail
At the jeers of a doubting crew,
Or dare you, whether you win or fail,
Strike out for a goal that's new?

EDGAR A. GUEST

CAN'T

A great, achieving soul will not clog itself with a cowardly thought or a cowardly watchword. Cardinal Richelieu in Bulwer Lytton's play declares: "In the lexicon of youth, which fate reserves for a bright manhood, there is no such word as 'fail.'" "Impossible," Napoleon is quoted as saying, "is a word found only in the dictionary of fools."

Can't is the worst word that's written or spoken;
Doing more harm here than slander and lies;
On it is many a strong spirit broken,
And with it many a good purpose dies.
It springs from the lips of the thoughtless each morning
And robs us of courage we need through the day:
It rings in our ears like a timely-sent warning
And laughs when we falter and fall by the way.

IT CAN BE DONE

Can't is the father of feeble endeavor,
The parent of terror and half-hearted work;
It weakens the efforts of artisans clever,
And makes of the toiler an indolent shirk.
It poisons the soul of the man with a vision,
It stifles in infancy many a plan;
It greets honest toiling with open derision
And mocks at the hopes and the dreams of a man.
Can't is a word none should speak without blushing;
To utter it should be a symbol of shame;
Ambition and courage it daily is crushing;
It blights a man's purpose and shortens his aim.
Despise it with all of your hatred of error;
Refuse it the lodgment it seeks in your brain;
Arm against it as a creature of terror,
And all that you dream of you some day shall gain.

Can't is the word that is foe to ambition,
An enemy ambushed to shatter Your will;
Its prey is forever the man with a lesson.
And bows but to courage and patience and skill.
Hate it, with hatred that's deep and undying,
For once it is welcomed 'twill break any man;

IT CAN BE DONE

Whatever the goal you are seeking, keep trying
And answer this demon by saying: "I can."

EDGAR A. GUEST

THE FIRM OF GRIN AND BARRETT

It has been said that when disaster overtakes us, we can do one of two things: we can grin and bear it, or we needn't grin. The spirit that keeps a smile on our faces when our burden is heaviest is the spirit that will win in the long run. Many men know how to take success quietly, the real test of a man is the way he takes failure.

No financial throe volcanic
Ever yet was known to scare it;
Never yet was any panic
Scared the firm of Grin and Barrett.
From the flurry and the fluster,
From the ruin and the crashes,
They arise in brighter lustre,
Like the phoenix from his ashes.
When the banks and corporations
Quake with fear, they do not share it;
Smiling through all perturbations

IT CAN BE DONE

Goes the firm of Grin and Barrett.
Grin and Barrett,
Who can scare it?
Scare the firm of Grin and Barrett?

When the tide-sweep of reverses
Smites them, firm they stand and dare it.
Without wailings, tears, or curses,
This stout firm of Grin and Barrett.
Even should their house go under
In the flood and inundation,
Calm they stand amid the thunder
Without noise or demonstration.
And, when sackcloth is the fashion,
With a patient smile they wear it,
Without petulance or passion,
This old firm of Grin and Barrett.
Grin and Barrett,
Who can scare it?
Scare the firm of Grin and Barrett?

When the other firms show dizziness,
Here's a house that does not share it.
Wouldn't you like to join the business?
Join the firm of Grin and Barrett?
Give your strength that does not murmur,

IT CAN BE DONE

And your nerve that does not falter,
And you've joined a house that's firmer
Than the old rock of Gibraltar.
They have won a good prosperity;
Why not join the firm and share it?
Step, young fellow, with celerity;
Join the firm of Grin and Barrett.
Grin and Barrett,
Who can scare it?
Scare the firm of Grin and Barrett?

SAM WALTER FOSS

UNAFRAID

I have no fear. What is in store for me
Shall find me ready for it, undismayed.
God grant my only cowardice may be
Afraid - to be afraid!

EVERARD JACK APPLETON

IT CAN BE DONE

THE TRAINERS

To Franklin, seeking recognition and aid for his country at the French court, came news of an American disaster. "Howe has taken Philadelphia," his opponents taunted him. "Oh, no," he answered, "Philadelphia has taken Howe." He shrewdly foresaw that the very magnitude of what the British had done would lull them into overconfidence and inaction, and would stir the Americans to more determined effort. Above all, he himself was undisturbed; for to the strong-hearted, trials and reverses are instruments of final success.

My name is Trouble I'm a busy bloke-
I am the test of Courage - and of Class-
bind the coward to a bitter yoke,
I drive the craven from the crowning pass;
Weaklings crush before they come to fame;
But as the red star guides across the night,
I train the stalwart for a better game;
I drive the brave into a harder fight.

My name is Hard Luck-the wrecker of rare dreams-
I follow all who seek the open fray;
I am the shadow where the far light gleams
For those who seek to know the open way;
Quitters break before they reach the crest,

IT CAN BE DONE

But where the red field echoes with the drums,
I build the fighter for the final test
And mold the brave for any drive that comes.

My name is Sorrow-I shall come to all
To block the surfeit of an endless joy;
Along the Sable Road I pay my call
Before the sweetness of success can cloy;
And weaker souls shall weep amid the throng
And fall before me, broken and dismayed;
But braver hearts shall know that I belong
And take me in, serene and unafraid.

My name's Defeat - but through the bitter fight,
To those who know, I'm something more than friend;
For I can build beyond the wrath of might
And drive away all yellow from the blend'
For those who quit, I am the final blow,
But for the brave who seek their chance to learn
I show the way, at last, beyond the foe,
To where the scarlet flames of triumph burn.

GRANTLAND RICE

IT CAN BE DONE

BATTLE CRY

We should win if we can; but in any case we should prove our manhood by fighting.

More than half beaten, but fearless,
Facing the storm and the night;
Breathless and reeling but tearless,
Here in the lull of the fight,
I who bow not but before thee,
God of the fighting Clan,
Lifting my fists, I implore Thee,
Give me the heart of a Man!

What though I live with the winners
Or perish with those who fall?
Surley the cowards are sinners,
Fighting the fight is all.
Strong is my foe - he advances!
Snapt is my blade, O Lord!
See the proud banners and lances!
Oh, spare me this stub of a sword!

Give me no pity, nor spare me;
Calm not the wrath of my Foe.
See where he beckons to dare me!

IT CAN BE DONE

Bleeding, half beaten - I go.
Not for the glory of winning,
Not for the fear of the night;
Shunning the battle is sinning-
Oh, spare me the heart to fight!

Red is the mist about me;
Deep is the wound in my side;
"Coward" thou criest to flout me?
O terrible Foe, thou hast lied!
Here with my battle before me,
God of the fighting Clan,
Grant that the woman who bore me
Suffered to suckle a Man!

JOHN G. NEIHARDT

IF YOU CAN'T GO OVER OR UNDER, GO AROUND

Often the straight road to the thing we desire is blocked. We should not then weakly give over our purpose, but should set about attaining it by some indirect method. A politician knows that one way of getting a man's vote is to please the

IT CAN BE DONE

man's wife, and that one way of pleasing the wife is to kiss her baby.

A baby mole got to feeling big,
And wanted to show how he could dig;
So he plowed along in the soft, warm dirt
Till he hit something hard, and it surely hurt!
A dozen stars flew out of his snout;
He sat on his haunches, began to pout;
Then rammed the thing again with his head-
His grandpap picked him up half dead.
"Young man," he said, "though your pate is bone,
You can't butt your way through solid stone.
This bit of advice is good, I've found:
If you can't go over or under, go round."

A traveler came to a stream one day,
And because it presumed to cross his way,
And wouldn't turn round to suit his whim
And change its course to go with him,
His anger rose far more than it should,
And he vowed he'd cross right where he stood.
A man said there was a bridge below,
But not a step would he budge or go.
The current was swift and the bank was steep,
But he jumped right in with a violent leap.

IT CAN BE DONE

A fisherman dragged him out half-drowned:
"When you can't go over-or under, go round."

If you come to a place that you can't get through,
Or over or under, the thing to do
Is to find a way round the impassable wall,
Not say you'll go YOUR way or not at all.
You can always get to the place you're going,
If you'll set your sails as the wind is blowing.
If the mountains are high, go round the valley;
If the streets are blocked, go up some alley;
If the parlor-car's filled, don't scorn a freight;
If the front door's closed, go in the side gate.
To reach your goal this advice is sound:
If you can't go over or under, go round!

JOSEPH MORRIS

A PRAYER

Garibaldi, the Italian patriot, said to his men: "I do not promise you ease; I do not promise you comfort. I promise you hardship, weariness, suffering; but I promise you victory."

IT CAN BE DONE

I do not pray for peace,
Nor ask that on my path
The sounds of war shall shrill no more,
The way be clear of wrath.
But this I beg thee, Lord,
Steel Thou my heart with might,
And in the strife that men call life,
Grant me the strength to fight.
I do not pray for arms,
Nor shield to cover me.
What though I stand with empty hand,
So it be valiantly!
Spare me the coward's fear questioning
wrong or right:
Lord, among these mine enemies,
Grant me the strength to fight.

I do not pray that Thou
Keep me from any wound,
Though I fall low from thrust and blow,
Forced fighting to the ground;
But give me wit to hide
My hurt from all men's sight,
And for my need the while I bleed,
Lord, grant me strength to fight.
I do not pray that Thou

IT CAN BE DONE

Shouldst grant me victory;
Enough to know that from my foe
I have no will to flee,
Beaten and bruised and banned,
Flung like a broken sword,
Grant me this thing for conquering-
Let me die fighting, Lord!

THEODOSIA GARRISON

THE MAN WHO FRETS AT WORLDLY STRIFE

"Lord, what fools these mortals be," exclaims Puck in, "A Midsummer Night's Dream." And well might the fairy marvel who sees folk vexing themselves over matters that nine times out of ten come to nothing. Much wiser is the man who smiles at misfortunes, even when they are real ones and affect him personally. Charles Lamb once cheerfully helped to hiss off the stage a play he himself had written.

The man who frets at worldly strife
Grows sallow, sour, and thin;
Give us the lad whose happy lift
Is one perpetual grin:

IT CAN BE DONE

He, Midas-like, turns all to gold-
He smiles when others sigh,
Enjoys alike the hot and cold,
And laughs though wet or dry.

JOSEPH RODMAN DRAKE

HEINELET

What sheer perseverance can accomplish, even in matters of the heart, is revealed in this little poem written in Heine's mood of mingled seriousness and gayety.

He asked if she ever could love him.
She answered him, no, on the spot.
He asked if she ever could love him.
She assured him again she could not.
He asked if she ever could love him.
She laughed till his blushes he hid.
He asked if she ever could love him.
At last, she admitted she did.

GAMALIEL BRADFORD

IT CAN BE DONE

ON DOWN THE ROAD

Hazlitt said that the defeat of the Whigs could be read in the shifting and irresolute countenance of Charles James Fox, and the triumph of the Tories in Pitt's "aspiring nose." The empires of the Montezumas are conquered by men who, like Cortez, risk everything in the enterprise and make retreat impossible by burning their ships behind them.

Hold to the course, though the storms are about you;
Stick to the road where the banner still flies;
The devil and his legions are ready to rout you-
Give 'em both barrels - and aim for their eyes.

Life's not a rose bed, a dream or a bubble,
A living in clover beneath cloudless skies;
And the devil hates a fighter who's looking for trouble,
So give 'im both barrels - and shoot for the eyes.

Fame never comes to the loafers and sitters,
Life's full of knots in a shifting disguise;
The devil only picks on the cowards and quitters,
So give 'em both barrels - and aim for the eyes.

GRANTLAND RICE

IT CAN BE DONE

CO-OPERATION

"We must all hang together, or assuredly we shall all hang separately," Benjamin Franklin is reported to have said at the signing of the Declaration of Independence.

> *It ain't the guns nor armament,*
> *Nor funds that they can pay,*
> *But the close co-operation,*
> *That makes them win the day.*
>
> *It ain't the individual,*
> *Nor the army as a whole,*
> *But the everlasting team-work*
> *Of every bloomin' soul.*

J. MASON KNOX

FOUR THINGS

What are the qualities of ideal manhood? Various people have given various answers to this question. Here the poet states what qualities he thinks are indispensable.

IT CAN BE DONE

Four things a man must learn to do
If he would make his record true:
To think without confusion clearly;
To love his fellow-men sincerely;
To act from honest motives purely;
To trust in God and Heaven securely.

HENRY VAN DYKE

IF

The central idea of this poem is that success comes from self control and a true sense of the values of things. In extremes lies danger. A man must not lose heart because of doubts or opposition, yet he must do his best to see the grounds for both. He must not be deceived into thinking either triumph or disaster final; he must use each wisely - and push on. In all things he must hold to the golden mean. If he does, he will own the world, and even better, for his personal reward he will attain the full stature of manhood.

If you can keep your head when all about you
Are losing theirs and blaming it on you,
If you can trust yourself when all men doubt you,
But make allowance for their doubting too;

IT CAN BE DONE

If you can wait and not be tired by waiting,
Or being lied about, don't deal in lies,
Or being hated don't give way to hating,
And yet don't look too good, nor talk too wise:

If you can dream - and not make dreams your master;
If you can think - and not make thoughts your aim,
If you can meet with Triumph and Disaster
And treat those two imposters just the same;
If you can bear to hear the truth you've spoken
Twisted by knaves to make a trap for fools,
Or watch the things you gave your life to, broken,
And stoop and build 'em up with worn-out tools:

If you can make one heap of all your winnings
And risk it on one turn of pitch-and-toss,
And lose, and start again at your beginnings
And never breathe a word about your loss;
If you can force your heart and nerve and sinew
To serve your turn long after they are gone,
And so hold on when there is nothing in you
Except the Will which says to them: "Hold on!"
If you can talk with crowds and keep your virtue,
Or walk with Kings - nor lose the common touch,
If neither foes nor loving friends can hurt you,
If all men count with you, but none too much;

IT CAN BE DONE

If you can fill the unforgiving minute
With sixty seconds' worth of distance run,
Yours is the Earth and everything that's in it,
And-which is more - you'll be a Man, my son.

RUDYARD KIPLING

THE LION PATH

Admiral Dupont was explaining to Farragut his reasons for not taking his Ironclads into Charleston harbor. "You haven't given me the main reason yet," said Farragut. "What's that?" "You didn't think you could do it." So the man who thinks he can't pass a lion, can't. But the man who thinks he can can. Indeed he oftentimes finds that the lion isn't really there at all.

I dare not!-
Look! the road is very dark-
The trees stir softly and the bushes shake,
The long grass rustles, and the darkness moves
Here! there! beyond!
There's something crept across the road just now!
And you would have me go?
Go there, through that live darkness, hideous

IT CAN BE DONE

With stir of crouching forms that wait to kill?
Ah, look! See there! and there! and there again!
Great yellow, glassy eyes, close to the ground!
Look! Now the clouds are lighter I can see
The long slow lashing of the sinewy tails,
And the set quiver of strong jaws that wait
Go there? Not I! Who dares to go who sees
So perfectly the lions in the path?

Comes one who dares.
Afraid at first, yet bound
On such high errand all no fear could stay.
Forth goes he, with lions in his path.
And then?

He dared a death of agony-
Outnumbered battle with the king of beasts-
Long struggles in the horror of the night-
Dared, and went forth to meet - O ye who fear!
Finding an empty road, and nothing there-
A wide, bare, common road, with homely fields,
And fences, and the dusty roadside trees-
Some spitting kittens, maybe, in the grass.

CHARLOTTE PERKINS GILMAN

IT CAN BE DONE

GOOD INTENTIONS

Thinking you would like a square meal will not in itself earn you one. Thinking you would like a strong body will not, without effort on your part, make you an athlete. Thinking you would like to be kind or successful will not bring you gentleness or achievement if you stop with mere thinking. The arrows of intention must have the bow of strong purpose to impel them.

The road to hell, they assure me,
With good intentions is paved;
And I know my desires are noble,
But my deeds might brand me depraved,
It's the warped grain in our nature,
And St. Paul has written it true:
"The good that I would I do not;
But the evil I would not I do."
I've met few men who are monsters
When I came to know them inside;
Yet their bearing and dealings external
Are crusted with cruelty, pride,
Scorn, selfishness, envy, indifference,
Greed-why the long list pursue?
The good that they would they do not;
But the evil they would not they do.

IT CAN BE DONE

Intentions may still leave us beast-like;
With unchangeable purpose we're men.
We must drive the nail home-and then clinch it,
Or storms shake it loose again.
In things of great import, in trifles,
We our recreant souls must subdue
Till the evil we would not we do not
And the good that we would we do.

ST. CLAIR ADAMS

THE FIGHTING FAILURE

"I'm not a rabid, preachy, pollyanna optimist. Neither am I a gloomy grouch. I believe in a loving Divine Providence who expects you to play the game to the limit. Who wants you to hold tight to His hand, and Who compensates you for the material losses by giving you the ability to retain your sense of values, and keep your spiritual sand out of the bearings of your physical machine, if you'll trust and - 'Keep Sweet, Keep Cheerful, or else - Keep Still.'" - Everard Jack Appleton.

He has come the way of the fighting men,
and fought by the rules of the Game,

IT CAN BE DONE

And out of Life he has gathered -
What? A living, - and little fame,
Ever and ever the Goal looms near -
seeming each time worth while;
But ever it proves a mirage fair -
ever the grim gods smile.
And so, with lips hard set and white
he buries the hope that is gone,
His fight is lost - and he knows it is lost -
and yet he is fighting on.

Out of the smoke of the battle-
line watching men win their way,
And, cheering with those who cheer success
he enter again the fray,
Licking the blood and the dust from his lips,
wiping the sweat from his eyes,
He does the work he is set to do -
and "therein honor lies."
Brave they were, these men he cheered, -
theirs is the winners' thrill;
His fight is lost - and he knows it is lost -
and yet he is fighting still.

And those who won have rest and peace;
and those who died have more;

IT CAN BE DONE

But, weary and spent,
he can not stop seeking the ultimate score;
Courage was theirs for a little time, -
but what of the man who sees
That he must lose,
yet will not beg mercy upon his knees?
Side by side with grim Defeat,
he struggles at dusk or dawn,
His fight is lost - and he knows it is lost -
and yet he is fighting on.

Praise for the warriors who succeed,
and tears for the vanquished dead;
The world will hold them close to her heart,
wreathing each honored head,
But there in the ranks, soul-sick,
time-tried, he battles against the odds,
Sans hope, but true to his colors torn,
the plaything of the gods!
Uncover when he goes by,
at last! Held to his task by will
The fight is lost - and he knows it is lost -
and yet he is fighting still!

EVERARD JACK APPLETON.

IT CAN BE DONE

MY PHILOSOPHY

Though dogs persist in barking at the moon, the moon's business is not to answer the dogs or to waste strength placating them, but simply to shine. The man who strives or succeeds is sure to be criticized. Is he therefore to abstain from all effort? We are responsible for our own lives and cannot regulate them according to other people's ideas.

I allus argy that a man
Who does about the best he can
Is plenty good enough to suit
This lower mundane institute-
No matter ef his daily walk
Is subject fer his neghbor's talk,
And critic-minds of ev'ry whim
Jest all git up and go fer him!

It's natchurl enugh, I guess,
When some gits more and some gits less,
Fer them-uns on the slimmest side
To claim it ain't a fare divide;
And I've knowed some to lay and wait,
And git up soon, and set up late,
To ketch some feller they could hate
For gain' at a faster gait.

IT CAN BE DONE

My doctern is to lay aside
Contensions, and be satisfied:
Jest do your best, and praise er blame
That follers that, counts jest the same.
I've allus noticed grate success
Is mixed with troubles, more er less,
And it's the man who does the best
That gits more kicks than all the rest.

JAMES WHITCOMB RILEY

WORK

The dog that dropped his bone to snap at its reflection in the water went dinnerless. So do we often lose the substance - the joy - of our work by longing for tasks we think better fitted to our capabilities.

Let me but do my work from day to day,
In field or forest, at the desk or loom,
In roaring market-place or tranquil room;
Let me but find it in my heart to say,
When vagrant wishes beckon me astray,
"This is my work; my blessing, not my doom;

IT CAN BE DONE

Of all who have, I am the one by whom
This work can best be done in the right way."

Then shall I see it not too great, nor small,
To suit my spirit and to prove my powers;
Then shall I cheerful greet the laboring hours,
And cheerful turn, when the long shadows fall
At eventide, to play and love and rest,
Because I know for me my work is best.

HENRY VAN DYKE

WISHING

Horace Greeley said that no one need fear the editor who indulged in diatribes against the prevalence of polygamy in Utah, but that malefactors had better look out when an editor took up his pen against abuses in his own city. We all tend to begin our reforms too far away from home. The man who wishes improvement strongly enough to set to work on himself is the man who will obtain results.

Do you wish the world were better?
Let me tell you what to do.
Set a watch upon your actions,

IT CAN BE DONE

Keep them always straight and true.
Rid your mind of selfish motives,
Let your thoughts be clean and high.
You can make a little Eden
Of the sphere you occupy.

Do you wish the world were wiser?
Well, suppose you make a start,
By accumulating wisdom
In the scrapbook of your heart;
Do not waste one page on folly;
Live to learn, and learn to live.
If you want to give men knowledge
You must get it, ere you give.

Do you wish the world were happy?
Then remember day by day
Just to scatter seeds of kindness
As you pass along the way,
For the pleasures of the many
May be ofttimes traced to one,
As the hand that plants an acorn
Shelters armies from the sun.

ELLA WHEELER WILCOX

IT CAN BE DONE

TO THE MEN WHO LOSE

Here's to the men who lose!
What though their work be e'er so nobly planned,
And watched with zealous care,
No glorious halo crowns their efforts grand,
Contempt is failure's share.

Here's to the men who lose!
If triumph's easy smile our struggles greet,
Courage is easy then;
The king is he who, after fierce defeat,
Can up and fight again.

Here's to the men who lose!
The ready plaudits of a fawning world
Ring sweet in victor's ears;
The vanquished's banners never are unfurled-
For them there sound no cheers.

Here's to the men who lose!
The touchstone of true worth is not success;
There is a higher test-
Though fate may darkly frown, onward to press,
And bravely do one's best.

IT CAN BE DONE

Here's to the men who lose!
It is the vanquished's praises that I sing,
And this is the toast I choose:

"A hard-fought failure is a noble thing;
Here's to the men who lose!"

ANONYMOUS

YOUR MISSION

One of the most often-heard of sentences is: "I don't know what I'm to do in the world." Yet very few people are ever for a moment out of something to do, especially if they do not insist on climbing to the top of the pole and waving the flag, but are willing to steady the pole while somebody else climbs.

If you cannot on the ocean
Sail among the swiftest fleet,
Rocking on the highest billows,
Laughing at the storms you meet;
You can stand among the sailors,
Anchored yet within the bay,
You can lend a hand to help them

IT CAN BE DONE

As they launch their boats away.
If you are too weak to journey
Up the mountain, steep and high,
You can stand within the valley
While the multitudes go by;
You can chant in happy measure
As they slowly pass along-
Though they may forget the singer,
They will not forget the song.

If you cannot in the harvest
Garner up the richest sheaves,
Many a grain, both ripe and golden,
Oft the careless reaper leaves;
Go and glean among the briars
Growing rank against the wall,
For it may be that their shadow
Hides the heaviest grain of all.

If you cannot in the conflict
Prove yourself a soldier true;
If, where fire and smoke are thickest,
There's no work for you to do;
When the battlefield is silent,
You can go with careful tread;
You can bear away the wounded,

IT CAN BE DONE

You can cover up the dead.
Go and toil in any vineyard,
Do not fear to do and dare.
If you want a field of labor
You can find it anywhere.

ELLEN M. H. GATES

BORROWED FEATHERS

Many good, attractive people spoil the merits they have by trying to be something bigger or showier. It is always best to be one's self.

A rooster one morning was preening his feathers
That glistened so bright in the sun; .
He admired the tints of the various colors
As he laid them in place one by one.
Now as roosters go he was a fine bird,
And he should have been satisfied;
But suddenly there as he marched along,
Some peacock feathers he spied.
They had beautiful spots and their colors were gay-
He wished that his own could be green;
He dropped his tail, tried to hide it away;

IT CAN BE DONE

Was completely ashamed to be seen.
Then his foolish mind hatched up a scheme-
A peacock yet he could be;
So he hopped behind a bush to undress
Where the other fowls could not see.
He caught his own tail between his bill,
And pulled every feather out;
And into the holes stuck the peacock plumes;
Then proudly strutted about.
The other fowls rushed to see the queer sight;
And the peacocks came when they heard;
They could not agree just what he was,
But pronounced him a funny bird.

Then the chickens were angry that one of their kind
Should try to be a peacock;
And the peacocks were mad that one with their tail
Should belong to a common fowl flock.
So the chickens beset him most cruelly behind,
And yanked his whole tail out together;
The peacocks attacked him madly before,
And pulled out each chicken feather.

And when he stood stripped clean down to the skin,
A horrible thing to the rest,

IT CAN BE DONE

He learned this sad lesson when it was too late-
As his own simple self he was best.

JOSEPH MORRIS

A POOR UNFORTUNATE

Things are never so bad but they might have been worse. An immigrant into the South paid a negro to bring him a wild turkey. The next day he complained: "You shouldn't shoot at the turkey's body, Rastus. Shoot at his head. The flesh of that turkey was simply full of shot." "Boss," said the negro, "dem shot was meant for me."

His hoss went dead an' his mule went lame;
He lost six cows in a poker game;
A harricane came on a summer's day,
An' carried the house whar' he lived away;
Then a airthquake come when that wuz gone,
An' swallered the lan' that the house stood on!
An' the tax collector, he come roun'
An' charged him up fer the hole in the groun'!
An' the city marshal - he come in view
An' said he wanted his street tax, too!

IT CAN BE DONE

Did he moan an' sigh? Did he set an' cry
An' cuss the harricane sweepin' by?
Did he grieve that his ol' friends failed to call
When the airthquake come an' swallered all?
Never a word o' blame he said,
With all them troubles on top his head!
Not him... He clumb to the top o' the hill-
Whar' standin' room wuz left him still,
An', barin' his head, here's what he said:
"I reckon it's time to git up an' git;
But, Lord, I hain't had the measels yit!"

FRANK L. STANTON

CLEAR THE WAY

Humanity is always meeting obstacles. All honor to the men who do not fear obstacles, but push them aside and press on. Stephenson was explaining his idea that a locomotive steam engine could run along a track and draw cars after It. "But suppose a cow gets on the track," some one objected. "So much the worse," said Stephenson, "for the cow."

Men of thought! be up and stirring,
Night and day;

IT CAN BE DONE

Sow the seed, withdraw the curtain,
Clear the way!
Men of action, aid and cheer them,
As ye may!
There's a fount about to stream,
There's a light about to gleam,
There's a warmth about to glow,
There's a flower about to blow;
There's midnight blackness changing
Into gray!
Men of thought and men of action,
Clear the way!

Once the welcome light has broken,
Who shall say
What the unimagined glories
Of the day?
What the evil that shall perish
In its ray?
Aid it, hopes of honest men;
Aid the dawning, tongue and pen;
Aid it, paper, aid it, type,
Aid it, for the hour is ripe;
And our earnest must not slacken
Into play.

IT CAN BE DONE

Men of thought and men of action,
Clear the way!

Lo! a cloud's about to vanish
From the day;
And a brazen wrong to crumble
Into clay!
With the Right shall many more
Enter, smiling at the door;
With the giant Wrong shall fall
Many others great and small,
That for ages long have held us
For their prey.
Men of thought and men of action,
Clear the way!

CHARLES MACKAY

THICK IS THE DARKNESS

How many of us forget when the sun goes down that it will rise again!

Thick is the darkness
Sunward, O, sunward!

IT CAN BE DONE

Rough is the highway-
Onward, still onward!
Dawn harbors surely
East of the shadows.
Facing us somewhere
Spread the sweet meadows.

Upward and forward!
Time will restore us:
Light is above us,
Rest is before us.

WILLIAM ERNEST HENLEY

CLEON AND I

Toward the end of the yacht race in which the *America* won her historic cup, the English monarch, who was one of the spectators, inquired: "Which boat is first?" "The *America* seems to be first, your majesty," replied an aide. "And which is second?" asked the monarch. "Your majesty, there seems to be no second." So it is in the race for happiness. The man who is natural, who is open and kind of heart, is always first. The man who is merely rich or sheltered or proud is not even a good second.

IT CAN BE DONE

Cleon hath a million acres, ne'er a one have I;
Cleon dwelleth in a palace, in a cottage I;
Cleon hath a dozen fortunes, not a penny I;
Yet the poorer of the twain is Cleon, and not I.

Cleon, true, possesses acres, but the landscape I;
Half the charm to me it yieldeth money cannot buy,
Cleon harbors sloth and dullness, freshening vigor I;
He in velvet, I in fustian, richer man am I.

Cleon is a slave to grandeur, free as thought am I;
Cleon fees a score of doctors, need of none have I;
Wealth-surrounded, care-environed, Cleon fears to die;
Death may come, he'll find me ready, happier man am I.

Cleon sees no charm in nature, in a daisy I;
Cleon hears no anthems ringing in the sea and sky;
Nature sings to me forever, earnest listener I;
State for state, with all attendants, who would change?
Not I.

CHARLES MACKAY

IT CAN BE DONE

MEETIN' TROUBLE

Some students of biology planned a trick on their professor. They took the head of one beetle, the body of another of a totally different species, the wings of a third, the legs of a fourth. These members they carefully pasted together. Then they asked the professor what kind of bug the creature was. He answered promptly, "A humbug." Just such a monstrosity is trouble - especially future trouble. Some things about it are real, but the whole combined menace is only an illusion, not a thing which actually exists at all. Face the trouble itself; give no heed to that idea of it which invests it with a hundred dire calamities.

Trouble in the distance seems all-fired big
Sorter makes you shiver when you look at it a-comin';
Makes you wanter edge aside, er hide, er take a swig
Of somethin' that is sure to set your worried head a-hummin'.
Trouble in the distance is a mighty skeery feller-
But wait until it reaches you afore you start to beller!

Trouble standin' in th' road and frownin' at you, black,
Makes you feel like takin' to the weeds along the way;
Wish to goodness you could turn and hump yerself straight back;

IT CAN BE DONE

Know 'twill be awful when he gets you close at bay!
Trouble standin' in the road is bound to make you shy-
But wait until it reaches you afore you start to cry!
Trouble face to face with you ain't pleasant, but you'll find
That it ain't one-ha'f as big as fust it seemed to be;
Stand up straight and bluff it out! Say, "I gotter a mind
To shake my fist and skeer you off-you don't belong ter me!"
Trouble face to face with you? Though you mayn't feel gay,
Laugh at it as if you wuz-and it'll sneak away!

EVERARD JACK APPLETON

MY CREED

We all have a philosophy of life, whether or not we formulate it. Does it end in self, or does it include our relations and our duties to our fellows? General William Booth of the Salvation Army was once asked to send a Christmas greeting to his forces throughout the world. His life had been spent in unselfish service; over the cable he sent but one word - OTHERS.

This is my creed: To do some good,
To bear my ills without complaining,
To press on as a brave man should

IT CAN BE DONE

For honors that are worth the gaining;
To seek no profits where I may,
By winning them, bring grief to others;
To do some service day by day
In helping on my toiling brothers.

This is my creed: To close my eyes
To little faults of those around me;
To strive to be when each day dies
Some better than the morning found me;
To ask for no unearned applause,
To cross no river until I reach it;
To see the merit of the cause
Before I follow those who preach it.

This is my creed: To try to shun
The sloughs in which the foolish wallow;
To lead where I may be the one
Whom weaker men should choose to follow.
To keep my standards always high,
To find my task and always do it;
This is my creed I wish that I
Could learn to shape my action to it.

S. E. KISER

BORROWING TROUBLE

It is bad enough to cry over spilt milk. But many of us do worse; we cry over milk that we think is going to be spilt. In line 1 sic=such; 2, a'=all; 3, nae=no; 4, enow=enough; 5 hae=have; sturt=fret, trouble.

> *But human bodies are sic fools,*
> *For a' their colleges an' schools,*
> *That when nae real ills perplex them,*
> *They mak enow themsels to vex them;*
> *An' ay the less they hae to sturt them,*
> *In like proportion less will hurt them.*

ROBERT BURNS

CHARACTER OF A HAPPY LIFE

"I'd rather be right than President," said Henry Clay. It is to men who are animated by this spirit that the greatest satisfaction in life comes. For true blessedness does not lie far off and above us. It is close at hand. Booker T. Washington once told a story of a ship that had exhausted its supply of fresh water and signaled its need to a passing vessel. The reply was, "Send down your buckets where you are."

IT CAN BE DONE

Thinking there was some misunderstanding, the captain repeated his signal, only to be answered as before. This time he did as he was bidden and secured an abundance of fresh water. His ship was opposite the mouth of a mighty river which still kept its current unmingled with the waters of the ocean.

> *How happy is he born and taught*
> *That serveth not another's will;*
> *Whose armor is his honest thought*
> *And simple truth his utmost skill!*
>
> *Whose passions not his masters are,*
> *Whose soul is still prepared for death,*
> *Not tied unto the world with care*
> *Of public fame or private breath;*
>
> *Who envies none that chance doth raise*
> *Or vice; who never understood*
> *How deepest wounds are given by praise*
> *Nor rules of state, but rules of good;*
>
> *Who hath his life from rumors freed,*
> *Whose conscience is his strong retreat;*
> *Whose state can neither flatterers feed,*
> *Nor ruin make accusers great;*

IT CAN BE DONE

Who God doth late and early pray
More of his grace than gifts to lend;
And entertains the harmless day
With a well-chosen book or friend;

This man is freed from servile bands
Of hope to rise or fear to fall;
Lord of himself, though not of lands;
And having nothing, yet hath all.

SIR HENRY WOTTON

SLOGAN

Some men want ideal conditions with pay in advance before they will work. But the world does not want such men, and has little place for them.

Don't prate about what is your right,
But bare your fists and show your might:
Life is another man to fight
Catch as catch can.

Don't talk of Life as scurvy Fate,
Who gave you favors just too late,

IT CAN BE DONE

Or Luck who threw you smiles for bait
Before he ran.

Don't whine and wish that you were dead,
But wrestle for your daily bread,

And afterward let it be said
"He was a man."

JANE M'LEAN

SMILES

Smiles bring out the latent energies within us, as water reveals the bright colors in the stone it flows over.

Smile a little, smile a little,
As you go along,
Not alone when life is pleasant,
But when things go wrong.
Care delights to see you frowning;
Loves to hear you sigh;
Turn a smiling face upon her,
Quick the dame will fly.

IT CAN BE DONE

Smile a little, smile a little,
All along the road;
Every life must have its burden,
Every heart its load.
Why sit down in gloom and darkness,
With your grief to sup?
As you drink Fate's bitter tonic
Smile across the cup.

Smile upon the troubled pilgrims
Whom you pass and meet;
Frowns are thorns, and smiles are blossoms
Oft for weary feet.
Do not make the way seem harder
By a sullen face,
Smile a little, smile a little,
Brighten up the place.

Smile upon your undone labor;
Not for one who grieves
O'er his task, waits wealth or glory;
He who smiles achieves.
Though you meet with loss and sorrow
In the passing years,

IT CAN BE DONE

Smile a little, smile a little,
Even through your tears.

ELLA WHEELER WILCOX

KEEP A-GOIN'!

Some men fail and quit. Some succeed and quit. The wise refuse to quit, whether they fail or succeed.

If you strike a thorn or rose,
Keep a-goin'!
Ef it hails, or ef it snows,
Keep a-goin'!
'Taint no use to sit an' whine,
When the fish ain't on yer line;
Bait yer hook an' keep a-tryin'-
Keep a-goin'!

When the weather kills yer crop,
Keep a-goin'!
When you tumble from the top,
Keep a-goin'!
S'pose you're out of every dime,
Bein' so ain't any crime;

IT CAN BE DONE

Tell the world you're feelin' prime-
Keep a-goin'!

When it looks like all is up,
Keep a-goin'!
Drain the sweetness from the cup,
Keep a-goin'!
See the wild birds on the wing,
Hear the bells that sweetly ring,
When you feel like sighin' sing-
Keep a-goin'!

FRANK L. STANTON

THE HOUSE BY THE SIDE OF THE ROAD

This poem has as its keynote friendship and sympathy for other people. It is a paradox of life that by hoarding love and happiness we lose them, and that only by giving them away can we keep them for ourselves. The more we share, the more we possess. We of course find in other people weaknesses and sins, but our best means of curing these are through a wise and sympathetic understanding.

IT CAN BE DONE

There are hermit souls that live withdrawn
In the peace of their self-content;
There are souls, like stars, that dwell apart,
In a fellowless firmament;
There are pioneer souls that blaze their paths
Where highways never ran;
But let me live by the side of the road
And be a friend to man.

Let me live in a house by the side of the road,
Where the race of men go by
The men who are good and the men who are bad,
As good and as bad as I.
I would not sit in the scorner's seat,
Or hurl the cynic's ban;
Let me live in a house by the side of the road
And be a friend to man.

I see from my house by the side of the road,
By the side of the highway of life,
The men who press with the ardor of hope,
The men who are faint with the strife.
But I turn not away from their smiles nor their tears-
Both parts of an infinite plan;

IT CAN BE DONE

Let me live in my house by the side of the road
And be a friend to man.

I know there are brook-gladdened meadows ahead
And mountains of wearisome height;
And the road passes on through the long afternoon
And stretches away to the night.
But still I rejoice when the travelers rejoice
And weep with the strangers that moan,
Nor have I my house by the side of the road
Like a man who dwells alone.

Let me live in my house by the side of the road
Where the race of men go by-
They are good, they are bad, they are weak, they are strong,
Wise, foolish-so am I.

Then why should I sit in the scorner's seat
Or hurl the cynic's ban?
Let me live in my house by the side of the road
And be a friend to man.

SAM WALTER FOSS

INDEX BY AUTHORS

A

ADAMS, ST. CLAIR.
Born in Arkansas, 1883. University education; European travel; has resided at one time or another in nearly all sections of America. Miscellaneous literary and editorial work. Wanted, a Man, 32; Good Intentions, 76.

ANONYMOUS.
Keep On Keepin' On, 29; Hope, 42; To the Men Who Lose, 84.

APPLETON, EVERARD JACK.
Born at Charleston, W. Va., Mar. 24, 1872. Very little schooling, but had advantages of home literary influences and a good library; at seventeen went into newspaper work in his home town; later went to Cincinnati, and worked on the daily Tribune, then on the Commercial Gazette; later connected with the Cincinnati Times-Star. For five years he wrote daily column of verse and humor ; besides his newspaper work, he has written over one hundred and fifty stories, hundreds of poems, many songs, and innumerable jokes, jingles, cheer-up wall cards, and the like. Author of two books

of poetry, "The Quiet Courage" and "With the Colors." With such intense work his health broke down, and for a number of years he has been a chronic invalid, but his cheer and his faith are as bright as ever. Unafraid, 59; The Fighting Failure, 77; Meetin' Trouble, 96.

B

BRADFORD, GAMALIEL.
Born at Boston, Mass., Oct. 9, 1863; privately tutored till 1832; entered Harvard College 1882 but was obliged to leave almost immediately because of ill health. Contributor of essays and poems to various magazines; has a remarkable insight into the characters of historical figures, and in a few pages reveals their inner souls. Among his books are "Types of American Character," "A Pageant of Life," "The Private Tutor," "Between Two Masters" "Matthew Porter," "Lee, the American," "Confederate 'Portraits," "Union Portraits," "A Naturalist of Souls," and "Portraits of American Women." Heinelet, 69.

BURNS, ROBERT.
Born at Alloway, near Ayr, Scotland, Jan. 25, 1759; died at Dumfries, Scotland, July 21, 1796. Received little education; drudgery on a farm at Mt. Oliphant 1766-77; on a farm at Lochlea 1777-84, during which time there was a period of loose living and bad companionship; at the death of his father he and his brother Gilbert

rented Mossgiel farm near Mauchline, where many of his best poems were written; winter of 1786-7 he visited Edinburgh, and was received into the best society; winter of 1787-8 revisited Edinburgh but rather coolly received by Edinburgh society; 1788 married Jean Armour, by whom he had previously had several children. Took farm at Ellisland 1788; became an excise officer 1789. Removed to Dumfries 1791; later years characterized by depression and poverty. Some of his best-known poems are "The Holy Fair," "The Cotter's Saturday Night," and "Tam O'Shanter"; wrote many of the most popular songs in the English language. Borrowing Trouble, 99.

C

COOKE, EDMUND VANCE.

Born at Port Dover, Canada, June 5, J866. Educated principally at common schools. He began to give lecture entertainments 1893, and has been for years one of the most popular lyceum men before the public. Frequent contributor of poems, stories, and articles to the leading magazines. His poem "How Did You Die?" has attained a nation-wide popularity. Among his books are "Just Then Something Happened," "The Story Club," "Told to the Little Tot," "Chronicles of the Little Tot," "I Rule the House," "Impertinent Poems," "Little Songs for Two," "Rimes to be Read," "The Uncommon Commoner," and "A Patch of Pansies." How Did You Die? 37.

CROSBY, ERNEST HOWARD.
> Born at New York City, Nov. 4, 1856; died there Jan. 3, 1907. Graduated from University of New York 1876, and from Columbia Law School 1878; lawyer in New York 1878-89; judge of international court at Alexandria, Egypt, 1889-94; returned to New York 1894, and interested himself in social reform. Among his books are "Plain Talk in Psalm and Parable," "Captain Jenks, Hero," "Swords and Plowshares," "Tolstoi and His Message," and "Labor and Neighbor." Life and Death, 51.

D

DRAKE, JOSEPH RODMAN.
> Born at New York City, Aug. 7, 1795; died there Sept. 21, 1820. Author of "The Culprit Fay" and "The American Flag." The Man Who Frets at Worldly Strife, 68.

F

FOSS, SAM WALTER.
> Born at Candia, N. H., June 19, 1858; died in 1911. Graduated from Brown University 1882; editor 1883-93; general writer 1893-8; librarian at Somerville, Mass., from 1898; lecturer and reader of his own poems. Among his books are "Back Country Poems," "Whiffs from Wild Meadows," "Dreams in Homespun," "Songs

of War and Peace" and "Songs of the Average Man." The Firm of Grin and Barrett, 57; The House by the Side of the Road, 105.

G

GARRISON, THEODOSIA.
Born at Newark, N. J., 1874. Educated at private schools at Newark. Married Joseph Garrison of Newark 1898; married Frederick J . Faulks of Newark 1911. Among her books are "The Joy of Life, and Other Poems," "Earth Cry, and Other Poems," and "The Dreamers." A Prayer, 66.

GILMAN, CHARLOTTE PERKINS.
Born at Hartford, Conn., July 3, 1860. Excellent home instruction; school attendance scant; real education reading and thinking, mainly in natural science, history, and sociology. Writer and lecturer on humanitarian topics, especially along lines of educational and legal advancement. The Forerunner, a monthly magazine, entirely written by her, published for seven years from 1910. Among her publications are "In This Our World," "Women and Economics," "Concerning Children," "The Home," "Human Work," "The Yellow Wallpaper," "The Man-made World," "Moving the Mountain," "What Diantha Did," and "The Crux." The Lion Path, 74.

GUEST, EDGAR ALBERT.
　　Born at Birmingham, Eng., Aug. 20, 1881; brought to the United States 1891; educated in grammar and high schools of Detroit, Mich. Connected with the Detroit Free Press since 1895; syndicates a daily poem in several hundred newspapers. His books are "A Heap O' Livin'," "Just Folks," "Over Here," "Path to Home," and "When Day is Done." It Couldn't Be Done, 19; See It Through, 22; There Will Always Be Something to Do, 45; How Do You Tackle Your Work? 46; The Things That Haven't Been Done Before, 53; Can't, 55.

H

HENLEY, WILLIAM ERNEST.
　　Born at Gloucester, Eng., Aug. 23. 1849; died July II, 1903. Educated at the Crypt Grammar School at Gloucester. Afflicted with physical infirmity, and in hospital at Edinburgh 1874-an experience which gave the material for his "Hospital Sketches." Went to London 1877; edited London (a magazine of art) 1882-6; the Scots Observer (which became the National Observer) 1888-93; and the New Review 1893-8. Besides three plays which he wrote in collaboration with Robert Louis Stevenson, he is the author of "Views and Reviews," "Hospital Sketches," "London Voluntaries," and "Hawthorn and Lavender." Thick Is the Darkness, 93.

K

KIPLING, RUDYARD.

Born at Bombay, India, Dec. 30, 1865. Educated in England at United Service College; returned to India 1880; assistant editor of Civil and Military Gazette 1882-89; returned to England 1889; resided in the United States for several years; has traveled in Japan and Australasia. Received the Noble Prize for Literature 1907; honorary degrees from McGill University, Durham, Oxford, and Cambridge. Among his books are "Departmental Ditties," "Plain Tales from the Hills," "Under the Deodars," "Phantom 'Rickshaw," "Wee Willie Winkle," "Life's Handicap," "The Light That Failed," "Barrack-Room Ballads," "The Jungle Book," "The Second Jungle Book," "The Seven Seas," "Captains Courageous," "The Day's Work," "Kim," "Just So Stories," "Puck of Pook's Hill," "Actions and Reactions," "Rewards and Fairies," "Fringes of the Fleet," and "Sea Warfare." If, 72.

KISER, SAMUEL ELLSWORTH.

Born at Shippenville, Pa. Educated in Pennsylvania and Ohio. Began newspaper work in Cleveland, and from 1900 until 1914 was editorial and special writer for the Chicago Record-Herald. Noted for his humorous sketches, which have been widely syndicated. His poem "Unsubdued" is, like Henley's "Invictus," a splendid portrayal, of undaunted courage in the face of defeat. Among his books are "Georgie," "Charles the Chauffeur," "Love Sonnets of an Office Boy," "Ballads of the Busy Days," "Sonnets of a Chorus Girl," "The Whole Glad Year," and "The Land of Little Care." My Creed, 97.

KNOX, J. MASON.
Co-operation, 71.

M

MACKAY, CHARLES.
Born at Perth, Eng., Mar. 27, 1814; died at London, Dec. 24, 1889. Editor of the Glasgow Argus 1844-47 and of the Illustrated London News 1852-59; New York correspondent of the London Times during the Civil War. Clear the Way, 91; Cleon, and I, 94.

M'LEAN, JANE.
Slogan, 102.

MALLOCH, DOUGLAS.
Born at Muskegon, Mich., May 5, 1877. Common school education; reporter on the Muskegon Daily Chronicle 1886-1903; member of the editorial staff of the American Lumberman from 1903; associate editor' from 1910; contributes verse relating to the forest and lumber camps to various magazines; is called "The Poet of the Woods." He is author of "In Forest Land,"

"Resawed Fables," "The Woods," "The Enchanted Garden," and "Tote- Road and Trail." Be the Best of Whatever You Are, 21.

MALONE, WALTER.

Born in De Soto Co., Miss., Feb. 10, 1866; died May 18, 1915. Received the degree of Ph.B. from the University of Mississippi 1887; practised law at Memphis, Tenn., 1887-97; literary work in New York City 1897-1900; then resumed law practice at Memphis; became Judge of second Circuit Court, Shelby Co., Tenn., 1905, and served till his death. Annual exercises held in the Capleville schools in his honor. An excellent edition of his poems, issued under the direction of his sister, Mrs. Ella Malone Watson of Capleville, Tenn., is published by the John P. Morton Co., of Louisville, Ky. Opportunity, 48.

MARKHAM, EDWIN.

Born at Oregon City, Ore., Apr. 23, 1852. Went to California 1857; worked at farming and blacksmithing, and herded cattle and sheep, during boyhood. Educated at San Jose Normal School and two Western colleges; special student in ancient and modern literature and Christian sociology; principal and superintendent of schools in California until 1899. Mr. Markham is one of the most distinguished of American poets and lecturers. His poem "The Man with the Hoe" in his first volume of poems is world-famous, and has been heralded by many as "the battle-cry of the next thousand years." He has sounded in his work the note of universal brotherhood and humanitarian interest, and has been credited as opening up a new school of American poetry appealing to the social conscience, where Whitman appealed only to the social consciousness. His books are "The Man with the Hoe, and Other Poems," "Lincoln, and Other Poems," "The Shoes of Happiness, and Other Poems," and "Gates of Paradise, and Other Poems." His book "California the Wonderful" is a volume of beautiful prose giving a historical, social, and literary study of the state. Preparedness, 51.

MASON, WALT.
Born at Columbus, Ontario, May 4, 1862. Self educated. Came to the United States 1880; was connected with the Atchison Globe 1885-7; later with Lincoln, Neb., State Journal; editorial paragrapher of the Evening News, Washington, 1893; with the Emporia, Kan., Gazette since 1907. Writes a daily prose poem which is syndicated in over two hundred newspapers, and is believed to have the largest audience of any living writer. Among his books are "Rhymes of the Range," "Uncle Walt," "Walt Mason's Business Prose Poems," "Rippling Rhymes," "Horse Sense," "Terse Verse," and "Walt Mason, His Book." The Welcome Man, 31.

MORGAN, ANGELA.
Born at Washington, D. C. Educated under private tutors and at public schools; took special work at Columbia University. Began early as a newspaper writer, first with

the Chicago American; then with the Chicago Journal, and New York and Boston papers. She is a member of the Poetry Society of America, The MacDowell Club, Three Arts, and the League of American Pen Women. She is one of the most eloquent readers before the public to-day; was a delegate to the Congress of Women at The Hague 1915, at which she read her poem "Battle Cry of the Mothers." Her four books of poems are "The Hour Has Struck," "Utterance, and Other Poems," "Forward, March!" and "Hail, Man!" and a fifth is soon to be published. Her book of fiction "The Imprisoned Splendor" contains well-known stories ("What Shall We Do with Mother?" "The Craving," "Such Is the Love of Woman," and "The Making of a Man"), some of which appeared previously in magazines. A novel is shortly to be published. When God* Wants a Man, 24; Work, 34.

MORRIS, JOSEPH.
Born in Ohio 1889. College and university education; professor of English and lecturer on literary subjects; newspaper and magazine contributor; connected with publishing houses since 1917 in various editorial capacities. A Lesson from History, 39; If You Can't Go Over or Under, Go Round, 63; Borrowed Feathers, 88.

N

NEIHARDT, JOHN GNEISENAU.
Born near Sharpsburg, Ill., Jan. 8, 1881. Completed the scientific course at the Nebraska Normal College

1897; received the degree of Litt.D. from the University of Nebraska 1917. Declared Poet Laureate of Nebraska by a joint resolution of the Legislature, Apr. 1921, in recognition of the significance of the American epic cycle upon which he has been working for eight years. Winner of the prize of five hundred dollars offered by the Poetry Society of America for the best volume of poetry ("The Song of Three Friends") published by an American in 1919. Has been literary critic of the Minneapolis Journal since 1912. Among his books are "The Divine Enchantment," "The Lonesome Trail," "A Bundle of Myrrh," "Man-Song," "The River and I," "The Dawn-Builder," "The Stranger at the Gate," "Death of Agrippina," "Life's Lure," "The Song of Hugh Glass," "The Quest," "The Song of Three Friends," "The Splendid Wayfaring," and "Two Mothers." Battle Cry, 62.

R

RICE, GRANTLAND.

Born at Nashville, Tenn., Nov. 1, 1880. Attended Vanderbilt University. Worked as sporting writer on the Atlanta Journal; came to New York City in 1911 His sporting column, "The Sportlight," is said to be more widely syndicated and more widely read than any other writing on topics of sport in the United States. Irvin S. Cobb says that it often reaches the height of pure literature, and as a writer of homely, simple American verse Grantland Rice is held by many to be the logical successor to James Whitcomb Riley. He is author of

"Songs of the Stalwart" and editor of the American Golfer. "Might Have Been," 43; The Trainers, 59; On Down the Road, 69.

RILEY, JAMES WHITCOMB.

Born at Greenfield, Ind., 1849; died at Indianapolis, Ind., July 22, 1916. Public school education; received honorary degree of M.A. from Yale 1902 ; Litt.D. from Wabash College 1903 and from the University of Pennsylvania 1904, and LL.D. from Indiana University 1907. Began contributing poems to Indiana papers 1873; known as the "Hoosier Poet," and much of his verse in the middle Western and Hoosier dialect. Among his books are "The Old Swimmin' Hole," "Afterwhiles," "Old Fashioned Roses," "Pipes o' Pan at Zekesbury," "Neighborly Poems," "Green Fields and Running Brooks," "Poems Here at Home," "Child-Rhymes," "Love Lyrics," "Home Folks," "Farm Rhymes," "An Old Sweetheart of Mine," "Out to Old Aunt Mary's," "A Defective Santa Claus," "Songs o' Cheer," "Boys of the Old Glee Club," "Raggedy Man," "Little Orphan Annie," "Songs of Home," "When the Frost Is on the Punkin," "All the Year Round," "Knee-Deep in June," "A Song of Long Ago," and "Songs of Summer." His complete works are issued by the Bobbs-Merrill Company in the "Biographical Edition of James Whitcomb Riley" 1913. My Philosophy, 80.

S

SILL, EDWARD ROWLAND.
>Born at Windsor, Conn., 1841; died at Cleveland, Ohio, Feb. 27, 1887. Graduated from Yale 1861; professor of English at University of California 1874-82. Opportunity, 49.

STANTON, FRANK LEBBY.
>Born at Charleston, S. C., Feb. 22, 1857. Common school education; served apprenticeship as printer; identified with the Atlanta press for years, especially with the Atlanta Constitution in which his poems have been a feature, and have won for him a unique place among modern verse writers. Some of his books are "Songs of the Soil," "Comes One With a Song," "Songs from Dixie Land," "Up from Georgia," and "Little Folks Down South." A Poor Unfortunate, 90; Keep A-Goin'! 104.

T

TEICHNER, MIRIAM.
>Born at Detroit" Mich., 1888. Educated in public schools there; graduated from Central High School; took special courses in English and economics at the University of Michigan. Member of staff of Detroit News after leaving school, writing a daily column of verse and humor; came to New York City as special feature writer of the

New York Globe 1915; in Germany for the Detroit News and Associated Newspapers writing of postwar social and economic conditions 1921. Victory, 28.

V

VAN DYKE, HENRY.

Born at Germantown, Pa., Nov. 10, 1852; graduated at Polytechnical Institute of Brooklyn 1869; A.B. degree from Princeton 1873; M.A. degree from there 1876 ; graduated from Princeton Theological Seminary 1877 ; studied at University of Berlin 1877-9; has received honorary degrees from Princeton, Harvard, Yale, Union, Wesleyan, Pennsylvania, and Oxford. Pastor of United Congregational Church, Newport, R. I., 1879-82, and of the Brick Presbyterian Church, New York, 1883-1900; professor of English literature at Princeton from 1900; U. S. minister to the Netherlands and Luxemburg 1913-17. Author of "The Poetry of Tennyson," "Sermons to Young Men," "Little Rivers," "The Other Wise Man," "The First Christmas Tree," "The Builders, and Other Poems," "The Lost Word," "Fisherman's Luck," "The Toiling of Felix, and Other Poems," "The Blue Flower," "Music, and Other Poems," "Out-of-Doors in the Holy Land," "The Mansion," and "The Unknown Quantity." Four Things, 72; Work, 82.

W

WILCOX, ELLA WHEELER.

Born at Johnston Centre, Wis., 1855; died at her home in Connecticut, Oct. 31, 1919. Educated at the University of Wisconsin. Among her books are "Maurine," "Poems of Pleasure," Worth While, 40; Wishing, 83; Smiles, 102.

"Kingdom of Love," "Poems of Passion," "Poems of Progress," "Poems of Sentiment, "New Thought Common Sense," "Picked Poems," "Gems from Wilcox," "Faith," "Love," "Hope," "Cheer," and "The World and I."

WOTTON, SIR HENRY.

Born at Bocton Malherbe, Kent, Eng., 1568; died at Eton, 1639. Educated at Winchester and Oxford; on the Continent 1588-95; became the secretary of the Earl of Essex 1595; English ambassador to Venice, Germany, etc.; became provost of Eton College 1624. Character of a Happy Life, 99.